"This is that rare thing: a book of lines that could never be written. Curated on the fly by Leslie McCollom—a remarkably talented arbiter of the absurd—the accidental wisdom, pathos, and beautiful honesty of schoolchildren here rings true and deep. To think that these words—these wicked punch lines to jokes that cannot exist—were nearly lost to the atmosphere is heartbreaking; to think that every hour of every day similar words are is sobering. Each line is a poem unto itself, the shortest of short stories, the catchphrase of a movement. Read at one go, it is nearly overwhelming in its unrelenting surprise; enjoy your first of many visits, and share this book with the few who are yet unfamiliar with this phenomenon of a project."

—Chris Onstad, author of *Achewood*

"Somewhere in the world, preschoolers are discussing the smell of whale breath, the necessity of breathing fire into toilets, the fact that some pants don't evaporate. From this kid-rarefied air, Leslie, with her pitch-perfect ears, plucks the best of these creative, off-kilter nuggets and writes them down. What results is proof that little innocents could and should run the world."

—Julia Suits, *New Yorker* cartoonist, author of
The Extraordinary Catalog of Peculiar Inventions,
and curator of @TweetsofOld

Preschool
Gems

Love, Death, Magic, and
Other Surprising Treasures from
the Mouths of Babes

Leslie McCollom

A Perigee Book

A PERIGEE BOOK
Published by the Penguin Group
Penguin Group (USA) Inc.
375 Hudson Street, New York, New York 10014, USA
Penguin Group (Canada), 90 Eglinton Avenue East, Suite 700, Toronto, Ontario M4P 2Y3,
Canada (a division of Pearson Penguin Canada Inc.) • Penguin Books Ltd., 80 Strand,
London WC2R 0RL, England • Penguin Group Ireland, 25 St. Stephen's Green, Dublin 2,
Ireland (a division of Penguin Books Ltd.) • Penguin Group (Australia), 250 Camberwell
Road, Camberwell, Victoria 3124, Australia (a division of Pearson Australia Group Pty. Ltd.)
• Penguin Books India Pvt. Ltd., 11 Community Centre, Panchsheel Park, New Delhi—110
017, India • Penguin Group (NZ), 67 Apollo Drive, Rosedale, Auckland 0632, New Zealand
(a division of Pearson New Zealand Ltd.) • Penguin Books (South Africa) (Pty.) Ltd.,
24 Sturdee Avenue, Rosebank, Johannesburg 2196, South Africa

Penguin Books Ltd., Registered Offices: 80 Strand, London WC2R 0RL, England

First edition: August 2012

Library of Congress Cataloging-in-Publication Data

McCollom, Leslie.
Preschool gems : love, death, magic, and other surprising treasures
from the mouths of babes / Leslie McCollom.
    p. cm.
"A Perigee book."
ISBN 978-0-399-53755-4 (pbk.)
1. Children—Quotations. 2. Children—Humor. I. Title.
PN6328.C5M45 2012
808'.6020209282—dc23   2012010969

PRINTED IN THE UNITED STATES OF AMERICA

10 9 8 7 6 5 4 3 2 1

To the children of New Day School

CONTENTS

INTRODUCTION

Preschool-aged children are essentially miniature Frankenstein's monsters. With no morality guiding their madly flailing limbs, they toddle about in a perpetual search for instant gratification and pleasurable sensory experiences. When they can't find these things, they fly into a destructive rage frenzy; when they do find them, they demand, "MORE, MORE!" and *then* fly into a destructive rage frenzy.

My job is to teach these creatures compassion for others, problem-solving skills, and songs about cleaning up after yourself; to transform instruments of nose picking into the tools of a master finger painter; to cultivate an appreciation for indoor plumbing; and basically just keep them alive for seven hours each school day until their brains become slightly more developed.

I am a preschool teacher.

Kids are a lot like dogs, really. After an egregiously unkind or shocking episode, they know how to hang their tails limply between their legs and look sorry. They walk over and brush their wet little noses against your hand and then wait the appropriate amount of time to start subtly wagging a little bit, until you aren't really mad anymore and you're just thinking about how cute they are, but they aren't actually sorry, because they don't understand what *sorry* means.

I've seen little kids do some messed-up stuff. They are bottomless pits of wants and needs. Unpredictable containers of human waste that often spill over at the least convenient moments. Small, sticky bullies. Now that I think about it, they're kind of rude, too. They don't hesitate to point out your least appealing physical traits or bring up embarrassing details, no matter who is around. They are tiny tyrants who scream at you or kick you while you're just trying to help them out.

They really are awful little creatures, children.

Or perhaps I'm being a bit harsh. I do see glimpses of humanity come shining through from time to time. When a child who can frequently be found eating leaves off a bush like an animal (no matter how many times you ask him to stop), hitting his classmates over the head with logs, or responding to every request with

"No!" all of a sudden gets close enough to you that you can smell his "clean baby" smell, looks straight into your eyes while drawing slow, openmouthed breaths and says, "Can I touch your face?" he suddenly doesn't seem like such a sociopath after all.

Actually, they're kind of cute. I really do sort of like them.

I like it when they are happy and they dance around, and the sound when they laugh is really quite pleasant. It's cool to watch the expression of wonderment cross their faces as they discover new things about the world, which happens on a daily, nay, hourly or even momentary basis.

It is so incredibly touching when one of them gives me a hug and says, "I love you, Teacher Leslie."

They renew my faith in humanity several times each day.

They are happy, skipping little gnomes. Lovely beings. Angels who have only recently descended from the celestial spheres, their minds still swirling in the cosmos.

Actually, they are great, and I love them all very much.

That's the thing about kids: They are both wonderful and terrible. In every way that they are far more troublesome and cruel than an adult, they are also exponentially more compassionate.

They are an amplification of all the good and bad things about human beings. They are like regular people, except the volume is turned up to eleven.

Since I started this job three years ago, I've been treated to a daily barrage of cracked wisdom. I quickly amassed an archive of startling brilliance and I decided I couldn't keep it from the world.

I started a Twitter feed, *Preschool Gems*, because every time I forgot one of their dazzling quotes, it felt like a precious jewel had slipped through my fingers. I couldn't believe the crazy things that popped out of their mouths—like "We're all just little babies in this world," and "Somebody pressed the 'never turn back to real me' button."

So, from the mouths of babes, I've collected the very best of two years of gems and have compiled them here, exactly as I found them, for your enjoyment and edification.

May you take them to heart.

—Leslie McCollom

Mythical Creatures

or "I'm Getting Kind of Confused,
I Do Believe in Fairies and I Don't
Believe in Fairies"

"OK, I have to go to the bathroom. Tell them that the password is 'blue dragon.' It's OK if I'm not here."

"Do you know about trolls? They're nice, but they live up in Norway and love stew."

"I need some water because I've been doing some unicorn tricks."

"I can't stop thinking about mermaids."

"I was in an igloo on a mountain. No yetis in there."

"OK, but I'm still a dragon."

"If I put the jewel in my mouth, then the fairies might not bring me another gift."

"Leprechauns are kind of like scientists."

"The fairies make me fairy pills."

"You wanna know how I know fairies are real? Because I am a fairy."

"Someone cast a spell on me so I can change into any animal, but I can never be a unicorn."

"There's no more elfs in my ear. They all went on vacation to my nose."

"I'm being a unicorn with my friend, but she needs to get her pants fixed first."

Looking Good

or "I Just Thought and Thought, and Then I Decided That I Would Be Glam"

"Is there pee on my cape?!"

"I got skinny jeans from Africa."

"My night costume has spots all over it."

"I've got the prettiest silly that you've ever seen."

"But my hat doesn't make me happy."

"I still have my haircut."

"My tinkernails are pink!"

"Guess what I want for Christmas? Makeup style guns and Hello Kitty stuff."

"Looks like everybody's having a button crisis!"

"I know someone who has golden pants. I also know someone who has leather pants."

"Don't touch me, only touch my Crocs."

"I have kitty socks at home and princess underwear on right now!"

"Wanna see what my pants can do?"

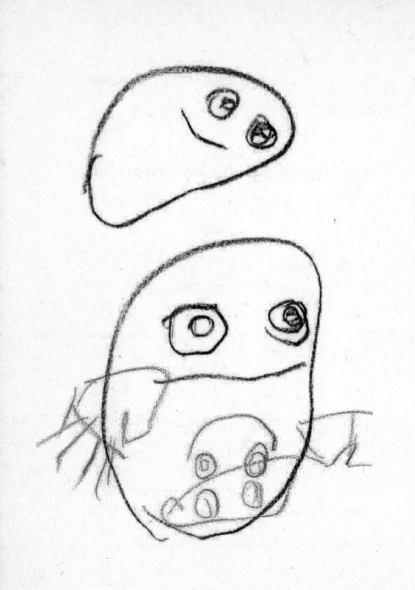

"Guess what! It's almost time to make hairdos!"

"I need to look very handsome today, do you know why? Because it's my celebration."

"That puddle looks like me."

"Aw, we were just talking 'bout rainbows and jackets."

"Here's your makeup saw!"

"These are my happy-mood shoes."

"You should get our phone number and come to my house and I'll put makeup on you."

"What's a mall?"

"I don't want my gloves to be dirty, I want to be a queen."

"Want me to make a ponytail to you?"

"I'm expensive."

The Wild Kingdom

or "One Hundred Lion Dads"

"Make me not a white tiger."

"It's not your dog's birthday, it's my dog's birthday."

"A whale comedian is a person who tells jokes to whales."

"I'm a grown-up pig who's drinking wine."

"Cows give us milk, chickens give us eggs, and otters give us seaweed."

"My tea smells like jaguars."

"There's a wolf in my tummy and a porcupine in my bum."

"I'm a big-kid raccoon in the bathroom."

"Baby ducks eat sauce."

"When I was a little boy I used to see chimpanzees at the North Pole."

"Us doggies!"

"But dinosaurs aren't cool because they're already dead, right?"

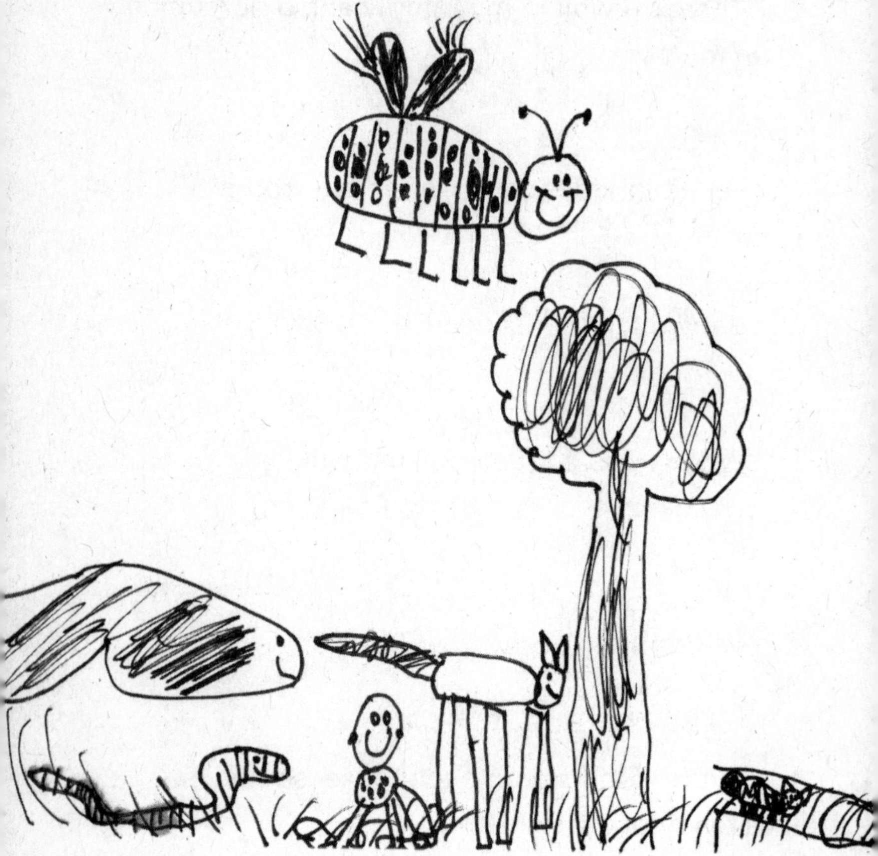

"I can't stand at the sink. I'm a cow, not a person."

"When wolves die they turn into dogs."

"Am dinosaur, and eat skin."

"I like to see dogs on the weekend."

"I made a gift for him, but he didn't see it because he's a dog and dogs don't see anything."

"My pony isn't in."

"Did you know that all ninjas are faster than cheetahs?"

"Whales and rockets are the best things."

"My brother's half penguin."

"If you go to Mexico, look for everything and see a lizard."

"I don't like dinosaurs and they don't exist."

"A sea urchin. That's my power animal."

"Do you know what, Dad? Chickens are verrry sensitive."

"I want to be a dolphin when I grow up."

"The dinosaurs tried their best not to eat people, but they just liked to eat people."

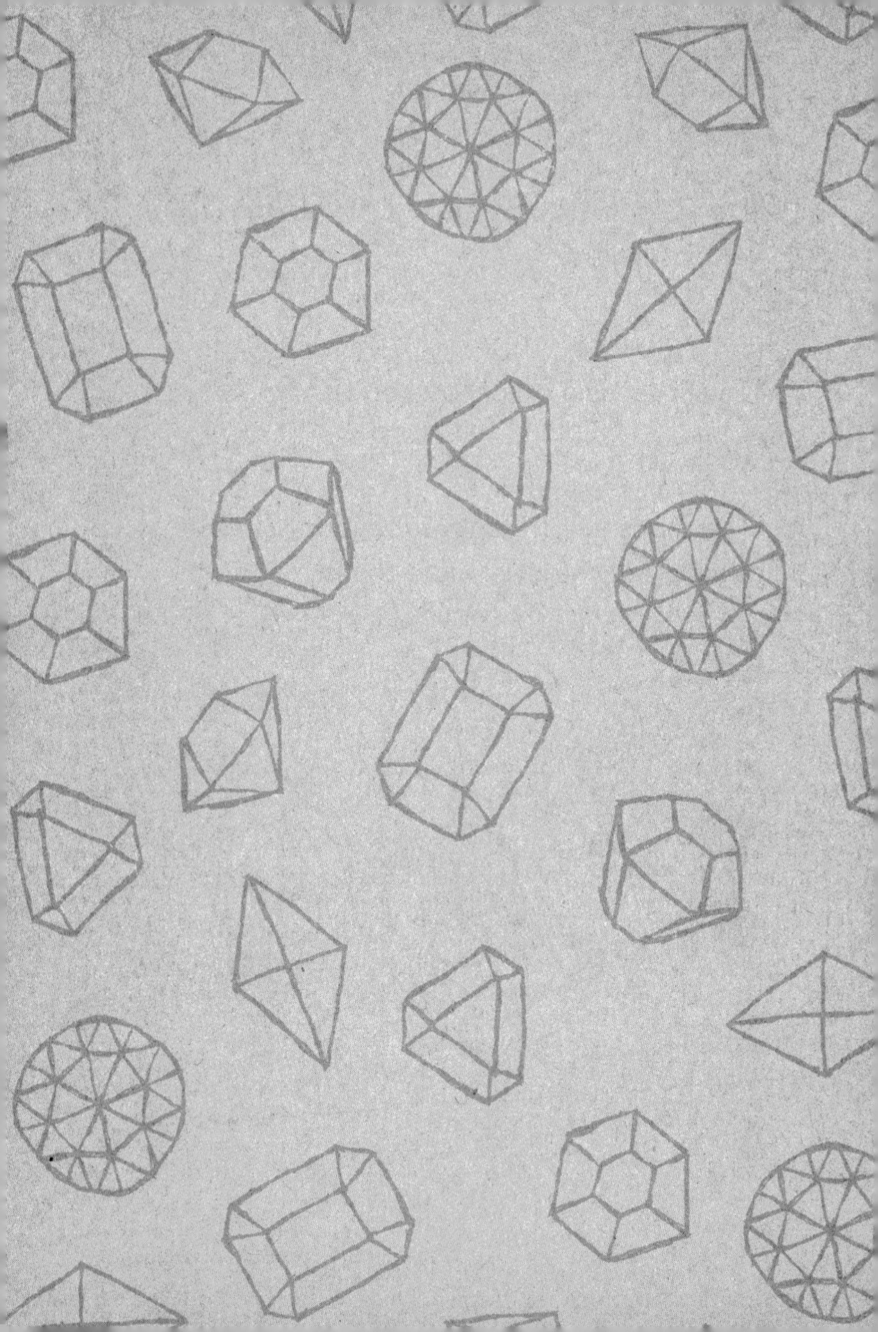

Having a Body

or "Something's Happening
with My Butt"

"Wanna know what kind of pee I made? It was orange."

"It's very wet. I peed in it a lot."

"Remember, you pee in my pee, OK?"

"I don't want to lick tongues with you today because I don't want to throw up in your mouth."

"Two times I get it in my nose."

"I can't pull up my pants because I'm a cracker, and crackers don't have any hands."

"Wanna taste my breath?"

"If you only eat rice, then you will be the tiniest kid at high school!"

"You're blooding."

"Big peepees are maybe like fountains."

"I just touched my eyeball for nine minutes!"

"I like it when people are naked."

"Touch his underpants butt."

"If I don't eat lunch, then my teeth will crumble and I won't get big and I'll never drive a car."

"Everyone has a nose. We talkin' about silly things."

"Guess what? I'm made of bones and blood."

"No one touches my privates but me. Other people can only touch my head and my brain."

"We have to do workouts so our backs stay fit and nice."

"I wish I were your bones. Then I would be warm."

"Actually everyone has a beard, it's just under their skin."

"Can I feel your big baby?"

"I always have a helper who's down on the floor. It's my foot!"

"Can I touch your neck?"

"You know what happens when you put feet and arms together? Feetarms."

"Could someone help me? I'm hungry, I got a wasp, and I got a headache!"

"I really miss my owie."

"Smell her breath, it's like a treat for the kids!"

"I get a Popsicle if I keep my underpants clean and dry."

"Whoa, I'm about to get hurt."

"Tell us a story from your brain."

Creativity and Deep Thoughts

or "Thinkin' 'bout Things in My Head, Thinkin' 'bout Cows"

"There's a stranger in my face."

"I need a break for my brain."

"Who are me?"

"Are people made of meat?"

"You're messing up my creation and it's going to be a disaster."

"In my dream I had a hot Popsicle."

"You know, the things that I make are very special."

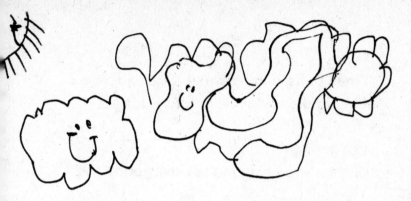

"I like all the colors except the colors of the rainbow."

"For real I'm not crazy."

"Don't build it with me because you might get it wrong and I might get upset."

"I'm too tired to touch someone's face."

"Let's talk about me."

"When I was in my mom's belly, I had a look at her future. I know your future, too."

"Change your eyes and see the world."

"One day I will tell the last of my jokes and then I will have to fill my body up with jokes again."

"Look at this music."

"Know what? I really, really, really . . . I forgot what I was going to say."

"My drawing is about snowmans for a good reason."

Familial Relations and Home Life

or "My Mom and My Dad and
My Friends and My Wife Are All
a Part of My Team"

"Do you like blue more than your mom?"

"Some big sisters are little tiny sisters."

"At home I'm even sillier. I take off my clothes."

"My mom asks me to not have a beard."

"Whoever's tummy we were in, that's who we can kiss."

"It's like this funny. It's as funny as my grandma loves me."

"Who goofed my mom?"

"Jack and the Beanstalk did have a dad, but they broke up."

"But we have all the babies that we wanted."

"I'm not going to get married, I'm just going to have a baby and then pretend to marry the baby."

"Soon I'm going to be a dad. 'Cause I'm four."

"When I grow up and my mom gets little, then she will be my baby."

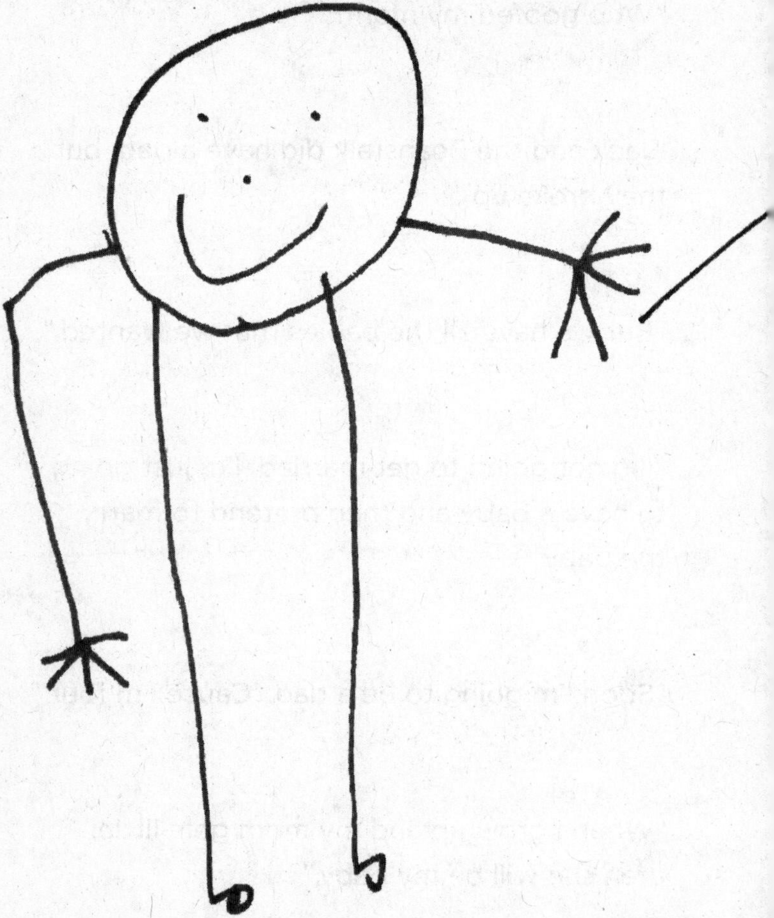

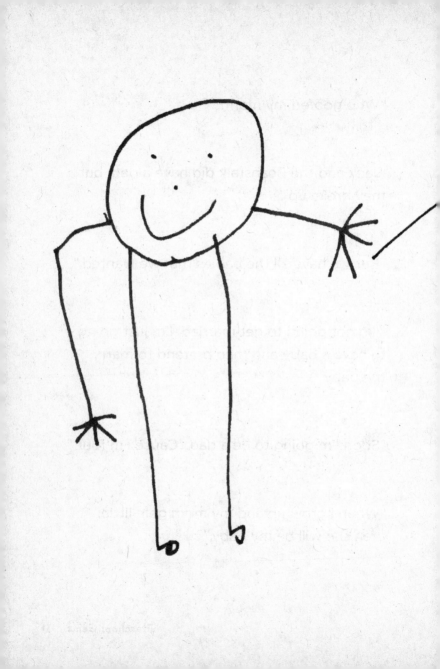

"Sometimes I say too many funny words at my home."

"Oh! This walnut shell is perfect for my grandma!"

"If you see a yellow house with a white door and a red curtain, that's my house!"

"My dad is thirteen. He has a dirt bike."

"My papa rides on a boy unicorn, and my mama and I ride on girl unicorns."

"My mom lived in the nineties."

"Don't hurt me, I'm my mom's little one."

"Jesus lives in a 'partment."

"At first I was a little frightened, but then I realized my mommy was still going to pick me up from school."

Magic and the Supernatural

or "Lots of Kids Can See Invisible Stuff"

"But there's a ghost in the sandbox, and he's activating the toys and turning them into traps!"

"Go computer! Go magic! Go flowers!"

"I'm just a guy with pixie dust."

"I mean, witches are real, but they live in another galaxy."

"I have lightning . . . in me!"

"I'm a nice woman ghost who's not going to hurt you or kill you."

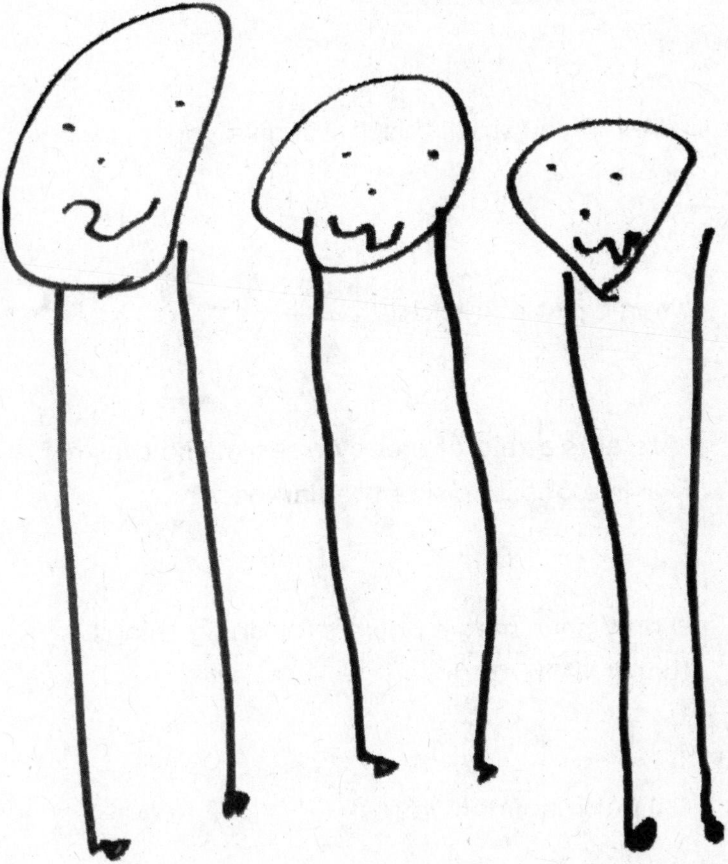

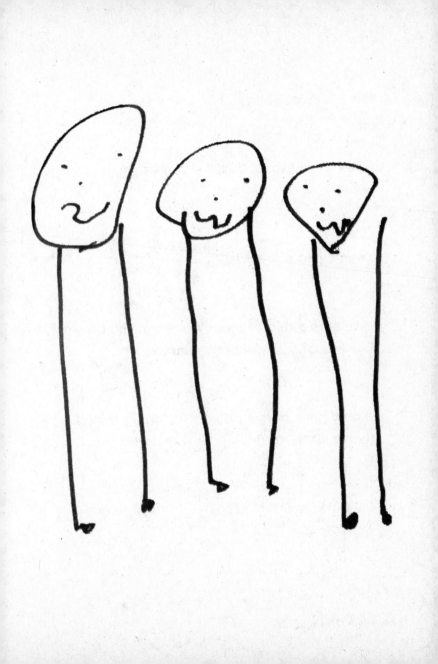

"I know five spells so far."

"Well, if you smell this, it will give you powers."

"Magic just magicked."

"Are ants afraid of creepy trees 'cause they're real live ghosts inside the darkness?"

"I only have magic powers for doing things that I WANT to do."

"I'll put magic on you."

"My powers are resting now."

"We live in a haunted house where all of the disappeared guys live."

"I'm half witch, half bear."

"This is a picture of a ghost showering, and his shower is our throw-up."

"Do you want some magic that will not make you dead?"

"Magic crystals in my head!"

"I'm a wizard boss."

"I only watch movies with a witch in them."

"No ghostses allowed at school!"

"I had a bad dream about all my teeth falling out, but my dreamcatcher catched it."

"Zombies aren't tornadoes, are they?"

The Dark Side

or "In the Nighttime I Turn Bad"

"We will become evil and the stars will come alive."

"I'm gonna get to jail all by myself."

"I can go even scarier."

"We're teenagers and we're spooking out."

"It's time for beasting."

"He's dead by a beast."

"I'm cutting off the doll's legs because I'm mad of her beauty."

"Um, can you be a nice troll?" "No."

"I'm taking you to locked in the dark land."

"Monsters have fierceness."

"I went to a wedding once. There were chain saws."

"I was born on the day of everything that's like monsters."

"Maybe our mom and dad turned to vampires."

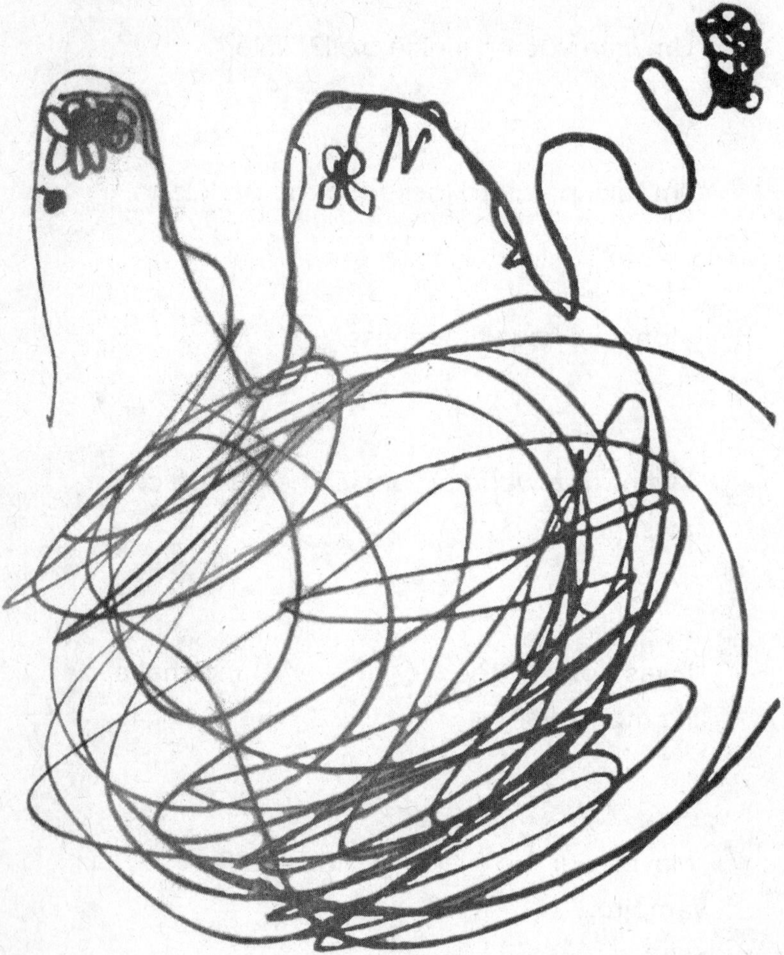

"I had a strong nightmare."

"The good force is like the main force. The evil force is like the second force. Don't use the evil force, just the good force."

"Blood is like tasty candy for me."

"I will tear the people of London apart."

"I don't know when my parents' anniversary is . . . Maybe it's when I die."

"And no one ever stopped screaming."

"I am the goddess of destruction!"

"Sorry, but your luck is doomed."

"Hey, let's talk about some more of *Star Wars*."

"I'm feeling poisonous, baby kitty."

"I want to make a sandbox out of her head."

"I had an accident. I did it on purpose."

"He said it was simple and it was good that I got hurt."

"I kicked her down the stairs a bit."

"A nightmare is when inside or outside you have a bad dream."

"I just like telling lies about myself."

"F***. Do you know about it?"

"When I grow up I'm going to be a firefighter so I can wear big boots so I can stomp on little animals."

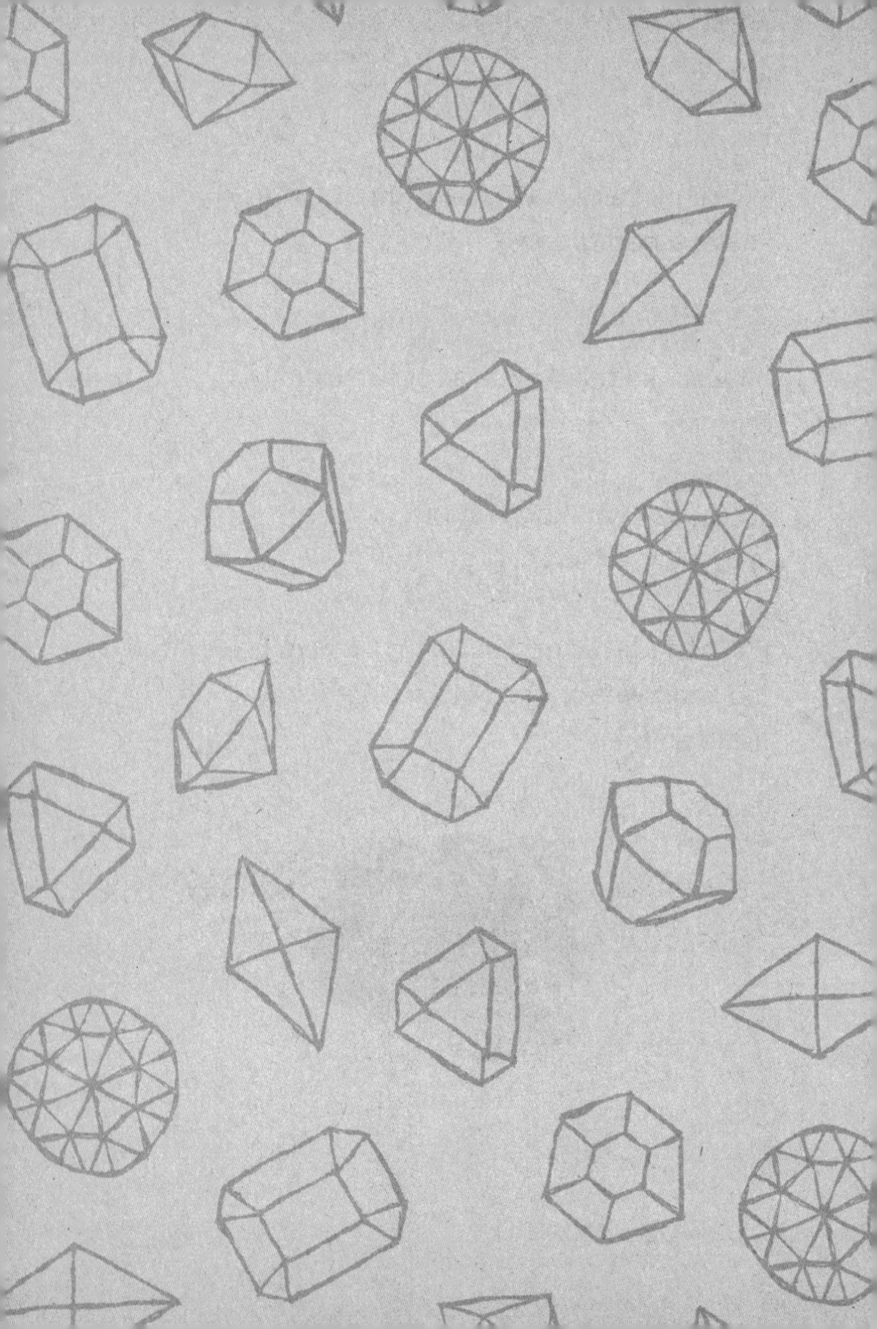

Love and Friendship

or "I Love Him, He's My
Favorite Kid Ever"

"How 'bout perhaps you forgot all about me, then you noticed me?"

"Are you still fallen in love with me?"

"I love David Bowie. I'm going to marry David Bowie."

"Does anyone want to be my boyfriend?"

"We love people, so we don't wanna kill 'em."

"You don't want a party with no friends!"

"If you want me to be your boyfriend, you're going to have to chase me."

"Bye! I'm your friend!"

"I'm looking for a friend who really wants to play with me."

"We two guys love every color of the rainbow."

"You can't kiss him, 'cause he's not real."

"I have a heart-shaped balloon at my house. Would you like to come over and see it sometime?"

"I kind of love everybody."

"I don't know where my favorite boy's going."

"I have a big huge dog. Could you come to my house today?"

"Your eyes look extra magical today."

"I remember when I didn't know you."

"I'm going to his real live house today."

"Bye, new friend!"

"I just don't like him! He's not cool, man."

"I know you're falling in love with me. I can tell."

"I dream about her two times."

"Wanna come hold hands in the sunshine?"

"When my birthday is on Friday you can come over to my house and I'll tell you all about my snow pants!"

"I would like for you to say 'wow' when I say that you can never be in love with me again."

"Our boyfriends never even share their knives."

"Hey, friends, come on in the club!"

"I like you, you're dressed up."

"You will have a baby because that's what girls do." "What do boys do?" "Not have babies at all."

"My big tall friend is coming in the summer."

"My friend's gonna paint me and then we're gonna go home."

"We have to save some, else there wouldn't be any more for the other childs!"

Snack Time

---

or "You Never Know When
You'll Get Lettuce"

"What should you do with people who don't have any ice cream?"

"Feed me pizza or I'll die."

"I have a chocolate chip cookie for real life."

"Tomorrow when you're cutting a sandwich you have to be careful, OK?"

"What even is a zucchini?"

"Last day we made some pizza. I got some trouble."

"Hot dogs and sing and dance around the fire. And pickles."

"We never make that, we don't have the 'gredients!"

"If you eat fughetti all night you'll turn into fughetti."

"And strawberries makes me be a princess!"

"Do you have any crackers at your house? And do you like them? And how are you doing?"

"How do a picture eat?"

"Candy goes into our body and makes us really happy."

"Everybody gonna eat me when I'm gonna be a strawberry."

"We eated smooshmellows at the hotel."

"We cooks pasketi 'cause we likes it."

"Who wants some strawberry chocolate? It's all free, you can get it from my head."

"My burrito doesn't have nothing in it."

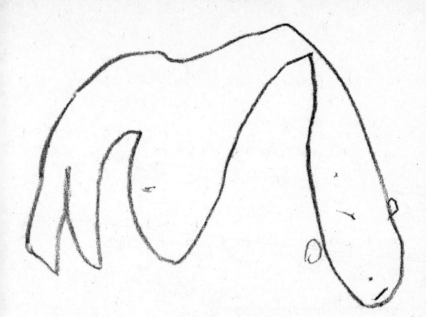

"It's almost time for eat everyone."

"I don't like kiwis, because they're not in season."

"I'm not a vegetarian, but when I'm not eating meat I am a vegetarian."

"I want to eat me up."

"I can't wait to get my mouth on those lentils."

"Could you put these herbs in my cubby?"

"These are strawbabies."

"Green gummy worms make my brain itch."

"I want to take a shower in soy sauce."

Life's Not Fair

or "The Birthday Girl Gets Everything! I Get NOTHING!"

"Now I'm so angry because no one's putting on my socks."

"I quit forever!"

"I don't wanna live! I don't wanna live this hard life anymore!"

"He says I can't have his air!"

"I don't like anybody trying to make me feel better."

"Today was a bad day. I got in chubble."

"They said my sunglasses look stupid, but they actually look cool. It made me sad. Actually, it made me heartbroken."

"There's no such thing as treasure."

"If you think my picture looks bad, then whatever!"

"He has the happiness of truth and I have the sadness."

"Sometimes I get knocked out. I lose my mind a little bit. My brain forgets things."

"I've been working on this paper watch for so long, it can do anything. It can even make me sad."

"It's just not fair! Everyone just has all these crystals and I don't have any!"

"I deserve to be punished!"

"I wish we could stay this young forever. I don't want to grow old and die."

"'Scuse me . . ." "We are not 'scusing you!"

"The people I work with are exhausting me."

What the ???

or "There Was a Lobster in
His Body and There Was Shrimps
All Over Him"

"There's no bumps in the sky really. You might see them in your mind but not up there."

"Teddy bear, tomato, water."

"OK, you guys are never gonna guess this so I'm just gonna tell you: basketball candies."

"There were ants in my eyes and they were working on computers."

"Sometimes my friend Spider-Man has congestion."

"Can I have my own pills tonight?"

"I know he have a mustache, but I don't know where is him."

"Did you have chicken pox?" "No, they stayed in their cave."

"I work at a restaurant who had a baby."

"Do you want to come in the hotel with me? It's gonna be really, really weird."

"My cheeks are pink . . . and are eat food and has toys. And crayons. Yeah."

"I made something different, like a coyote patch."

"Have you heard about manners camp where you learn about manners? It's a state of mind."

"Smelly armpits freak show."

"I'm filthy and I'm driving."

"We're lightning, you're just pineapple."

"People are hamburgers in America!"

"I had some emergency shoes, but I don't know where they went."

"I want to show you where my fire emergency is."

"I'm so over making these shoes."

"Is this the place where the fire comes out?"

"They're not funny things, they're bad things, and they get in your nose."

"What's sugar pants? What do you mean?"

"Instead of doing the dollars, I did quarters. And I did a lot of quarters."

"I'm building a dream tower that's made out of pee."

"Somebody pressed the 'never turn back to real me' button."

"That's not a knife, it's a stirrer for baby's vitamins."

"Do you know where I'm going for a few months? Nowhere. Because I made a potion out of my grandma's shoe, and I put it in my food."

The Big Picture

or "Remember What I Told You in the Bathroom: Life Is More Important Than Anything"

"Is today a long time?"

"When I'm an old man with a walking stick I'll still remember you . . . but you'll be dead."

"Is this preschool?"

"This isn't like taxi drivers to paradise or something. You have to get on your own horse and ride."

"I don't care about time-outs. I only care about my life."

"You have powers to make as much power as you want, and you never lose it."

"You know what's gonna happen to yourself."

"Life is but a bowl of nothing."

"When I get old I wanna disappear."

"Hey, universe, I'm gonna kick the heck out of you."

"So it started out as stardust, and then there were fish, then monkeys, then humans."

"Once, a long time ago, I had the whole world, and then I lost it."

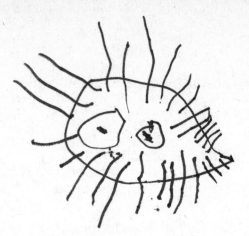

"Do you know how babies die? They grow up and they get old."

"No thing is prettier than any other thing."

"Which time is it?"

"Even though I'm a kid I'm kind of wise because I almost know about the whole earth."

"I love everything in the world, even fake stuff."

"I can look through people's bodies. I can see where the dinosaurs died."

"Then you will die and I will die and there will be no one else left in the world."

"We're all just little babies in this world."

"A good guy is someone who does be nice, but sometimes they get it all mixed up like a bad guy."

"We're all booby traps."

"Mr. Rogers is an old man that doesn't exist anymore."

"It was a long, long time ago. It was the day before this day."

"The hardest thing is remembering that I'm four."

"What even is this?"

"I need to want something."

"We're in the ocean, sister."

Rules and Society

or "I Want to Be That Deer
and Not Have Any Human Parents
or Laws"

"Since I'm at my house, I can take my pants off. When you get to your house you can take off your pants."

"I will not eat Play-Doh . . . but sometimes I will."

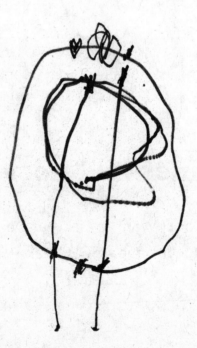

"We're pretending that we're people and we help other people, so they give us lots of money."

"Why were you making a sound?" "Because I'm a boy."

"What if there were no grown-ups and no Barack Obama, then we could be the chosen ones and everyone would wear shirts of our faces!"

"I have a cool trick, but it's not allowed."

"Can I touch your braid? No or yes?"

"No butts at school."

"I'm sitting here because I showed my underwear."

"Only girls can go down the pink line."

"You know what, you guys? When we grow up and get married and buy a house we're going to need a lot of money. A hundred of money."

"At the park there's, like, no laws."

"The people on TV are in charge of the snow."

"You aren't the boss of what I quit!"

"We're not saying you don't know how to play, we're just saying maybe you forgot how to play."

"When I grow up I want to be a Canadian."

"Why you didn't do it properly?"

"Make sure to get a raincoat that covers your vagina."

"If you forgot to wear underwear, that's OK. The teachers won't be mad at you."

"I know I'm a kid, but I'm not fired."

"Make sure I don't pee in these pants."

"First college, then space."

Make Believe

or "He's Pretending Pretend's Real"

"Watch out, I'm gonna get some dinner from the sky!"

"I pooped a fake story."

"Once upon a time there were only skeletons in the world."

"There's a bear over there in the bushes. It sells me things."

"Just for pretend life."

"One time, somewhere far away, someone got a job, then they fell asleep on a rainbow, then they died."

"And I didn't have a shirt on ever again."

"There's orange colors on your treasure, my dear."

"This story is called 'My Mother Kills Me Like Nothing.'"

"I've got two pretend friends comin' to my Easter egg hunt, and their names are Nothin' and Nobody."

"This isn't a gun, it's a picnic, and we were having a nice day till you said that!"

"Pretend this was a barf world where everyone barfed!"

"I'm chewing nothing gum."

"Um, she chopped my hand with a piece of bark because I said her pretend ice cream wasn't real? But also, I want some?"

"I'm a toy volcano!"

"Some tiny invisible aliens keep tying us up, and they're punching us! And they don't listen to people!"

"My friend is coming over for dinner tonight, but he doesn't exist."

"I glow in the dark and I am now a bobcat."

"We're flying to each other's homes and then we're gonna play peek-a-boo closet."

"He said that I'm his snack."

"Teacher, this tag says, 'Please let me go to the beach if I want to.'"

"One time the big bad wolf came to my house to bite us and I was like 'Hey! But I'm nice and I'm a girl!'"

"Some people don't like to be breathed with fire."

"Do you want to be the guard bunny? The guard bunny gets a sword."

"When I'm six I'm going to go to Paris all by myself! I'm going to ride a horse."

"We're downloading movies onto bark chips."

"I had a rock and it was special and it looked like teeth."

"She's just sitting there for a pretend-potty reason. I have to go pretend potty, too."

"This is not like a regular game because we're fighting crime for real."

"Some teachers get littler and littler till they're kids."

Don't Mess with Me

or "If You Want to Get Hit,
Then Stay Right Here"

"OK, sister. You have to go home."

"I peed in YOUR pants!"

"I know where my chair is, so just leave me alone."

"Let's give mean high fives."

"Now I'm gonna be mad at people."

"Get out of my world!"

"I'm about to say 'silence': Silence!"

"You're in the kicking zone."

"No, I'm not killed. I'm still alive."

"I'm gonna wreck this school apart."

"They were saying serious business to me."

"Tonight I'm going to my favorite place to eat and fight!"

"I'm totally bonked out."

"He was pretending to be a tiger and I didn't want him to be. So I hurt him."

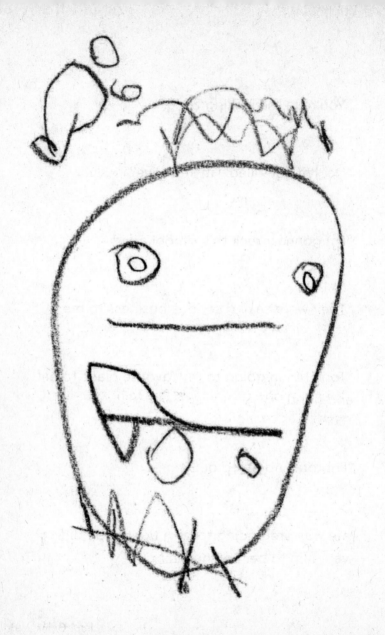

"This needs to get broken."

"We are kinda not talkin' about guns."

"Bigger kids like me are grouchy about pirates."

"May you stop roaring at me, please?"

"I drew a bad guy shooting a rainbow, but that's not very nice."

"I got a fairy gun."

"He plays tricks, and I don't like the tricks that he plays."

"Let's sword some stuff!"

"Stop bragging like you're the best."

"This is a monster cave, and I'm a monster."

"We are roarin' at that baby."

"I'm not allowed to play in volcanoes, but I'm not afraid of them."

"He said two bad words to me. He said 'bossy' and 'hush.'"

"When big kids punch they needs help."

"I have a haircut, so don't push it, OK?"

"You know what? Computers are super smart, but I can beat 'em."

"I'm not really into funny things right now."

"I'm just a girl like that."

"My skateboard shirt is my professional fire-chief truck shirt."

"I'm gonna tell my dad to cancel this school!"

Feeling Good

or "This Is My Favorite Day
of My Whole Life!"

"I never ever am going to frown on this day."

"Oh, thank you! Now there's even more wine than I expected!"

"Look at my cool, awesome pillow."

"Sometimes I just do these cool moves and then I change the cool moves into another kind of cool moves."

"I'm giddy-uppin'!"

"I saw a puddle in the shape of a heart and no one harmed me, so it was a good day."

"I like you got a cozy shirt!"

"Look at me—I'm skiing and I'm perfect and I love myself."

"I fell because I high-fived so hard."

"Parties? I love parties!"

"I want to go to the occasion!"

"You should be aware of my pretty moves."

"I'm a rock star! Look, I'm drinking cola!"

"The best score is when you win. That's the last score."

"Have a good dog!"

"Being happy is actually a good thing."

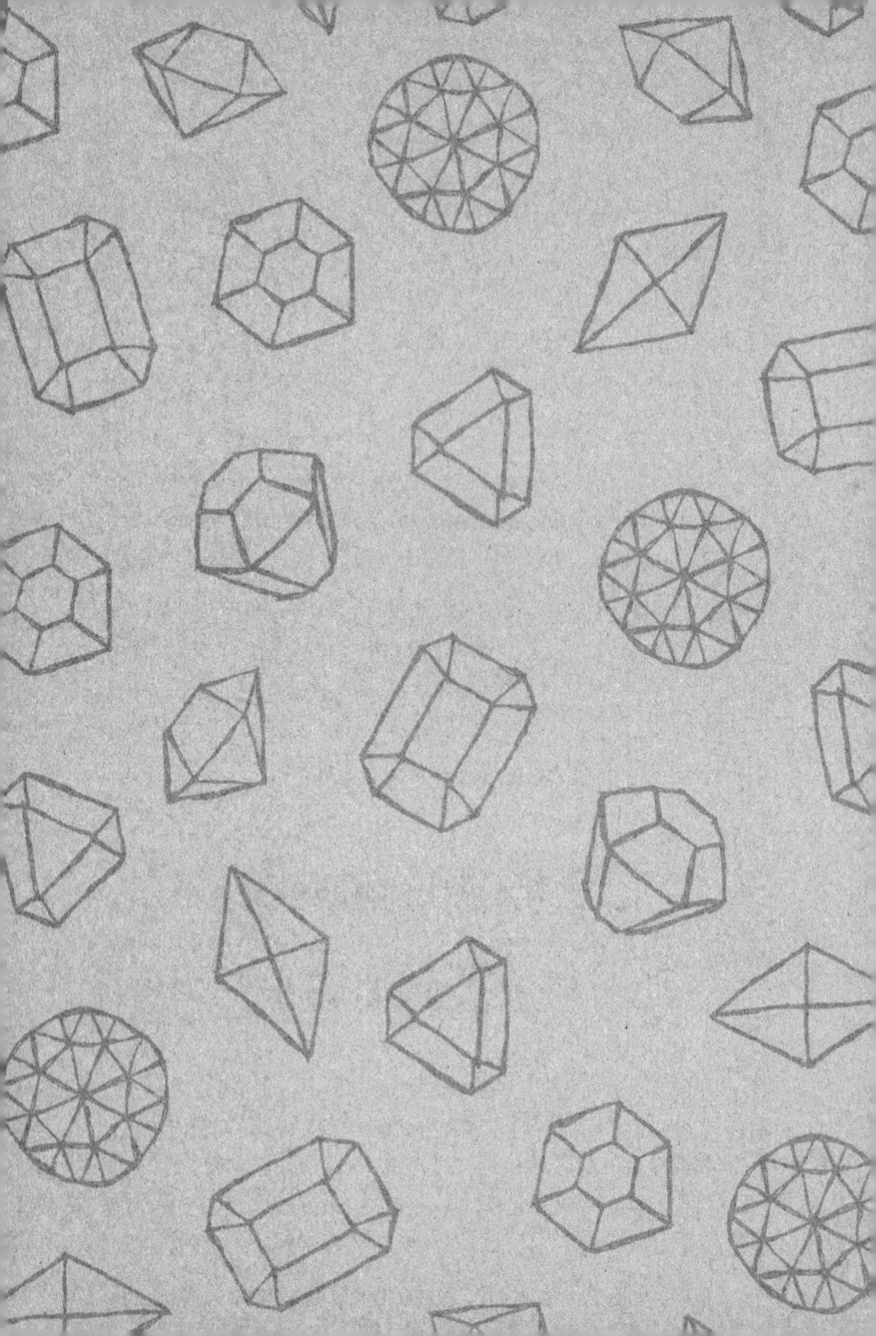

Letting Loose

---

or "Do Whatever You Want
as Pirates!"

"Can we do rock and roll for them?"

"I'm not wearing underwear for real life!"

"We're having a party at sixteen o'clock."

"I have a bunch of dirty dirty."

"OK, I'm going to drive my car to my crazy train now. It goes off the rails sometimes."

"I don't even know who is a rock star, I just like them."

"Teenagers pull their pants down."

"I washed my hands backwards!"

"My dad was told there would be a clown."

"I'm gonna see how long this button can stand here!"

"Strawberry naked sundae."

"I can't stop even jumping and galloping!"

"Ah, such a nice vacation in paradise away from capturing villains, and I am a so tired cowgirl."

ACKNOWLEDGMENTS

To my parents and to every teacher I ever had: Thank you. And also, I'm sorry.

To Mr. Rogers, the Muppets, camp, and grape Kool-Aid, for bringing great joy and meaning to my formative years.

To my fellow teachers, especially Patrick Dundon and Katie Walsh, for keeping their ears open.

To my friends and family, and my editors and agent, for the conversations we had that made this book possible.

To all my Internet friends: Thanks a million!

To Chris Fontaine, for lots of things.

Leslic

"ME"

I   I have brown hair to my shoulders. I am short. I Have a dog, a mom and dad and both of my goldfish are dead. Tragic isn't it though? I love pizza. My hobby is reading.

ABOUT THE AUTHOR

Leslie McCollom is a teacher and writer living in Portland, Oregon. She still loves pizza and reading.

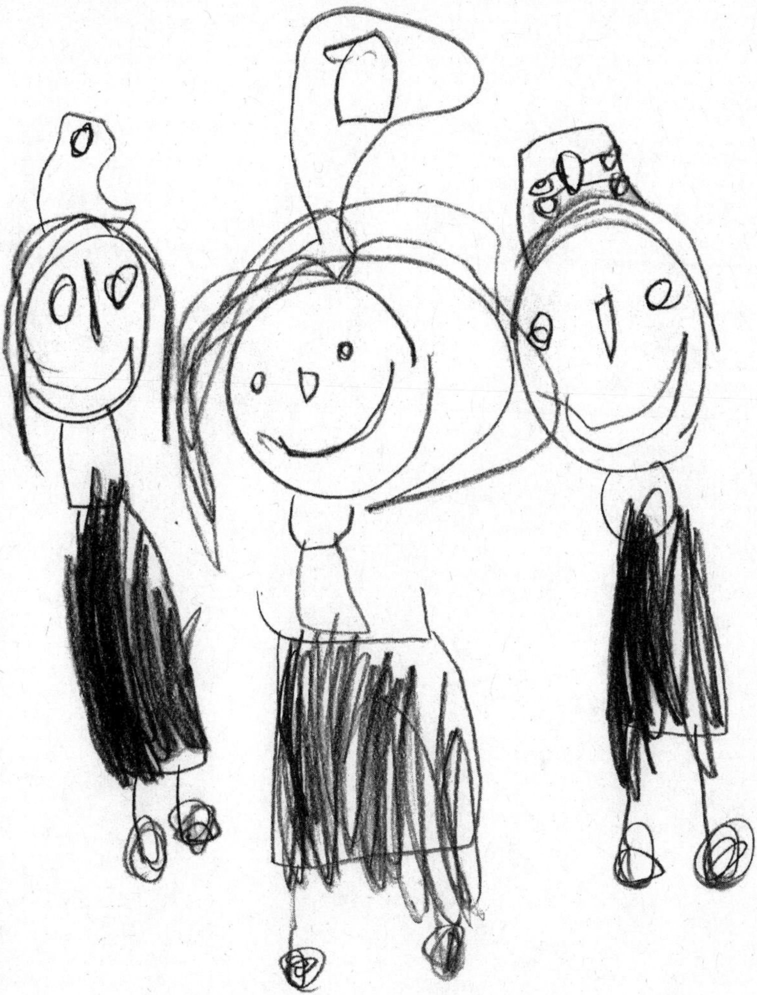